Change

Contents

People change 2

Animals change 4

Insects change 6

Plants change 8

Water changes 10

The weather changes 12

The Earth changes 14

Index 16

People change

age 3 months

age 4

People change as they grow from a baby to an adult. They grow bigger.

age 12   age 30   age 70

Their arms and legs grow much longer.
Their hair grows and changes colour.

Animals change

A chameleon can change the colour of its skin. It can change to match the colours around it.

It changes colour to hide from other animals. This is called camouflage.

Insects change

eggs

nymph

A dragonfly changes as it grows. A young dragonfly hatches from an egg. The young dragonfly is called a nymph.

When it is two years old, the nymph starts to change. It squeezes out of its skin. It becomes an adult dragonfly.

Plants change

poppy bud

Poppies change as they grow.
A poppy plant grows from a seed.
Buds grow on the plant. The buds
open out into flowers.

Seeds grow in each flower. When the flower dies, a seed box is left. The seeds are scattered by the wind.

Water changes

Water is a liquid which can change. It changes when it is heated. It changes when it is frozen.

Boiling

When water boils, it changes into a gas. The gas is called steam.

 Do not touch boiling kettles

Freezing

When water freezes, it changes into a solid. The solid is called ice.

The weather changes

The weather changes. Different seasons have different weather.

Sometimes it is warm and sunny.

Sometimes it is cold and wet.

The Earth changes

volcano

A volcano can change the surface of the Earth. When it erupts, a volcano shoots out ash, rocks and red hot lava.

Sometimes a volcano erupts under the sea. It grows so tall that the top comes out of the water. It forms a new island.

a
b
c
d
e
f
g
h
i
j
k
l
m
n
o
p
q
r
s
t
u
v
w
x
y
z

Index

 adult 2

 island 15

 baby 2

 nymph 6, 7

 bud 8

 seed box 9

 chameleon 4

 steam 11

 eggs 6

 volcano 14, 15

 ice 11

 weather 12

16